For 7 year olds who love football

Illustrations by Dan McCloskey

First published in Great Britain in 2023 by Bell & Mackenzie Publishing Limited

BELL & MACKENZIE
PUBLISHING LIMITED

REALLY FUN

FOOTBALL FACTS

For 7 Year Olds

Get ready for trivia overload! Bursting with fantastic football facts and amazing stats about the beautiful game.

Which Captain is also a brilliant golfer?

How many footballs would it take to reach Mars?

Which striker holds the record for the fastest ever hat-trick?

Which British legend has scored 260 goals?

Keep reading to find the answers to these and loads more really fun footie facts...

A 2016 football match in Brazil was interrupted when a capybara, the world's largest rodent, decided to take a nap on the field.

Manchester City Star Phil Foden joined the club when he was only 4 years old.

Some fans believe that a black cat crossing the pitch during a match is good luck.

But lucky for which team?

Paul the Octopus, who lived in Germany, was famous for helping predict results during the 2010 World Cup.

The Ballon d'Or is like the Oscars for footballers! It's an award given to the best football player in the world.

By the time Lionel Messi was 34, he had already won the Ballon d'Or 7 times!

In South Africa, fans use long, plastic horns called vuvuzelas which sound like a swarm of giant buzzing bees.

Brazilian player Pelé is considered one of the greatest players of all time. He scored over 1,000 goals in his career.

He was the first person to call football 'The Beautiful Game'.

Ronaldo is the ultimate social media superstar with more than 530 million Instagram followers, making him the most followed person in the world!

To keep his body in tip-top condition, Ronaldo eats six healthy meals every day.

In Italy, fans are known for creating massive displays using banners, flags and flares. These displays, known as "tifo" are world famous.

Did you know that the FIFA 12 video game holds a special record? It's the fastest selling sports game ever!

In the game the on-screen players you control have special skills...

..but sometimes, the real players don't agree with their stats in the game and complain on social media.

England Captain Harry Kane is a brilliant golfer.

He's almost good enough to go 'pro'. How cool is that?

At 38 years old, Italian hero Francesco Totti is the oldest player to score in the Champions League.

The ancient Roman army played a version of football known as "harpastum".

The soldiers loved it so much, they even played it to warm-up before battle.

The birthplace of modern football is England.

Before the Football Association was formed in 1863 there were no rules to follow.

The Women's England football team are called 'The Lionesses'.

'The 'Lionesses' beat Germany to win the Euros 2022.

It is estimated that there are more footballs in the world than there are people!

So even if everyone decided to play at the same time, there would still be enough balls to go around.

The Norway Cup is a huge
football tournament for kids from
all around the world.

Every year, over 1,000 teams
come together to play and have
fun. It's the biggest tournament
in the world.

Aged only 17 years and 40 days, Barcelona's Ansu Fati became the youngest player to ever score a Champions League goal.

CAMP NOU FC
BARCELONA

The Scilly Isles in UK have the tiniest soccer league in the whole world!

It's called the St. Mary's League and only has two teams.

Qatar built a brand new city called Lusail in the desert.

It cost them 37 billion pounds! They built it just for the final match of the 2022 World Cup.

To celebrate goals in Poland, fans turn their backs to the pitch and jump up and down together.

The most red cards ever given out in a single Premier League match is 3.

That happened in 2013 between Southampton and West Brom. It was a wild game!

Have you heard about the fastest ever goal in the Premier League?

It was like a lightning bolt, scored just 7.69 seconds after the game started between Watford v Southampton.

The first pair of football boots noted in history were made for King Henry VIII in 1526.

YE OLD FOOTBALL BOOTS

Old fashioned football boots were very different than the boots of today. They were really heavy and had thick, studded soles.

The boot leather would often become stiff and uncomfortable after getting wet, making it difficult to play in the rain.

Ex-Liverpool striker Sadio Mané made history by scoring the fastest hat-trick in the Premier League!

It only took him 2 minutes and 56 seconds to score 3 amazing goals against Aston Villa.

Some football players are so good at using their feet, they can do things like tie their shoelaces with their toes.

Former Manchester Utd boss Sir Alex Ferguson is the king of managers in the Premier League, with a record-breaking 810 games!

He still goes to see almost every match they play.

English footballer Levi Foster once got a yellow card for farting in the ref's face.

Alan Shearer is the king of goals in the Premier League! He has scored an amazing 260 times...

...which is the most of any player ever!

Before referees had whistles, they used handkerchiefs to signal fouls.

Cristiano Ronaldo is a super-scorer! He has scored more goals than anyone else in the whole world.

FIFA (the biggest football organisation) recognises him as the top scorer of all time!

The biggest football shirt-artwork ever was made using more than 20,000 shirts to create a picture of an eagle.

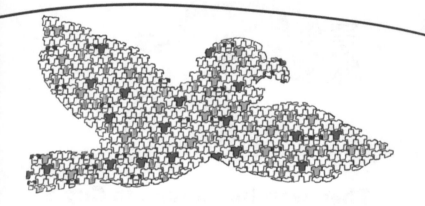

Real Madrid were like soccer ninjas in the 1950s, sneaking up on their opponents and scoring lots of goals!

They won the European Cup 5 times in a row, which doesn't happen very often.

Footie fans went opera-crazy during the 1990 Word Cup when Luciano Pavarotti's 'Nessun Dorma' went to #2 in the UK charts.

The Football Association actually tried to ban football for women in 1921.

Luckily that didn't last long and now women's football is played around the world by over 13 million women and girls.

The 1950 World Cup final was a huge showdown between Brazil and Uruguay!

Even though the stadium was only supposed to hold 173,850 people, lots more snuck in and there were almost 210,000 fans there!

Every season, all the teams in the Premier League score so many goals, it's like a never-ending goal celebration with an average of 1000+ goals per season!

Derby County had a rough ride in the 2007/08 season.

They won only 1 game and lost 29 - ouch! But, at least they made the other teams feel like champions!

Can you believe it? No English manager has ever won the Premier League!

The last time an English manager won the top division was way back in 1987.

But who knows, maybe an English manager will soon find the magic touch!

In some countries, fans bring their dogs to matches dressed up in team colours.

A man named Aaron Moon set the record for heading a ball 120 times in 60 seconds.

Recently however the Football Association has recommended that heading practice is limited.

The Premier League began in 1992. Before that the league was called the First Division.

 Manchester United

Chelsea

 Manchester City

In total only seven clubs have won the Premier League title:

Arsenal

Blackburn Rovers

Leicester City

Liverpool

Bayern Munich's stadium in Germany has a sliding roof that can be opened or closed depending on the weather!

Some footballer players can kick a ball at speeds of more than 100 km/h.

That's about the same as the maximum running speed of a cheetah!

Some teams have kits with special pockets for players to store their gum or mints during the game.

Red cards were first used in the 1970 World Cup as a way for referees to show players they were kicked out of the game.

It's not just players who can get shown red cards though. Managers can get yellow and red cards too!

England hero Gary Lineker once accidently pooed himself during a world cup match.

Manchester United's stadium Old Trafford is the biggest stadium in the Premier League.

Only Wembley Stadium, the national stadium, is bigger.

In South Africa, there's a football pitch that is made of recycled tyres!

In a recent match between USA and Honduras, temperatures dropped to -19c.

The goalkeeper was allowed to wear a balaclava which is normally against the rules.

It's not easy being a goalkeeper and sometimes they make comical mistakes...

... like accidentally scoring own goals or making silly errors that lead to goals.

Liverpool keeper Loris Karius had one of the world's worst games in 2018 when he made two huge mistakes which led to Real Madrid scoring twice in the Champions League final.

In 1891 in the USA a football was used to play the first ever game of basketball! Can you believe it?

A teacher wanted to give his students a fun indoor sport, so he made up the game of basketball and wrote down the rules.

Wembley stadium has a special VIP area for royalty and celebrities called the Royal Box.

The Premier League is the best league in the world, but not all teams can stay in it forever. Some teams get 'relegated'.

Think of it like a game of musical chairs, where the music stops and the teams with the fewest points has to give up their chair in the league.

The FA cup is the oldest football competition in the world.

Fans love the FA Cup because teams from lower leagues get to play against the top clubs.

Some prisons in the UK have football leagues for prisoners.

Professional football games use a standard size 5 ball.

The ball has 32 panels that are stitched together to form its round shape.

In the old days, shin pads looked like big blocks and were tied to the player's legs with straps.

Today, soccer shin pads are much lighter, more flexible and better at protecting players from hard tackles.

100!!!

Manchester City are the only club to score 100 points in the Premier League in a single season.

A football pitch must be like a giant, flat green carpet so that the ball can roll easily and players can run around without tripping.

There must be no more than a 1.5% slope, to make sure everyone has a fun and safe game.

The person in charge of the pitch is called a groundskeeper. He has one of the most important tasks in the team.

It's his job to keep the grass healthy so that's it's safe to play on and perfect for the players.

Can you imagine scoring a goal and then getting hurt because you're so excited about it?

It happens more often than you think, with more than 1 out of every 20 injuries on the field happening from goal celebrations.

You won't believe it, but Arsenal player Gabriel Magalhaes has lost the same tooth twice!

...and get this, it happened while playing against the same team, Brighton & Hove Albion!

Marcus Rashford made his professional debut for Manchester United in 2016, becoming the youngest player at the time to ever score for the club.

Have you ever had a string of bad luck? Well Sunderland FC can relate!

They hold the record for having the most losses in a row. Yep, you heard it right, 20 defeats in a row! Imagine playing 20 games and not winning a single one.

Imagine having a golden trophy so valuable and shiny, that people tried to steal it twice!

That's exactly what happened to the World Cup Trophy in 1966 and 1983.

But don't worry it was quickly found, and is now safely guarded by security guards at all times.

Some countries have their own unique football trophies, like the Scottish League Cup which is shaped like a giant bowl.

The Coppa Italia is shaped like a giant cupcake.

A football fan in Argentina has a collection of over 6000 football shirts,

...but he still wears the same one to every game!

In 2022, 15 year old Ethan Nwaneri became the youngest player ever to play Premier League football.

Football teams have special characters called mascots to make the games more fun and exciting for the fans.

Some team mascots are rabbits, lions, eagles and even super-heroes.

Jack Grealish broke the British transfer record when he joined Manchester City from Aston Villa for £100 million in 2021.

**Jack Grealish wears age 7-8
kids-sized shin pads.
He says they bring him good luck.**

Manchester City has the most expensive team in the whole world.

ONLY £2 BILLION

They have players who are worth almost 2 billion pounds.

Goalkeepers are allowed to hold the ball for a maximum of 6 seconds before they must release it back into play.

5-A-Side football is like the fast-moving cousin of normal football.

Instead of big teams and big fields, you only need 5 friends and a tiny patch of grass to have a manic kick about!

At 38 years old Chelsea's Thiago Silva is the oldest player currently playing in the Premier League.

Half-time snacks, whether sweet or savoury, add to the excitement of a football game and bring fans together!

In England, they eat pies.

In Germany, they eat sausages.

In Italy, they eat pizza.

 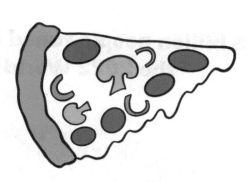

In Spain, they eat churros.

In France, they eat crepes.

5 billion people tuned in to watch the 2022 World Cup.

That's more than half of the world's population!

Spurs hero Harry Kane grew up in a family of Tottenham Hotspur fans and has been a fan of the club since he was a young boy.

Iranian football fan Arash Ahmadi Tifakani is super-talented!

He holds the world record for 'keeping-up' a football for 21.2 km, that's almost half a marathon!

Plus, he holds the record for balancing a football on his head for over 8 hours.

That's longer than most people sleep in a night!

Liverpool FC sell a fun version of hot dogs called Klopp Dogs.

...named after the team's highly successful manager Jürgen Klopp.

If you put 195 million footballs next to each other they would reach from Earth to Mars when they are at are closest to each other.

When Mars is further away from Earth it would take 1.4 trillion footballs...

...to go from one planet to the other!

Some football teams use dogs as ball-boys during matches.

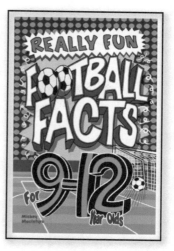

Also in the Really Fun Football Series.
Collect Them All!

Made in United States
Troutdale, OR
12/02/2023

15055956R00056